NOTES AND

FOR

OFFICERS.

ANTI-AIRCRAFT CORPS

OF THE

ROYAL NAVAL AIR SERVICE.

LONDON DIVISION.

Published and © by the
The Naval & Military Press
in association with the Royal Armouries

Unit 10 Ridgewood Industrial Park,
Uckfield, East Sussex, TN22 5QE
Tel: +44 (0) 1825 749494
Fax: +44 (0) 1825 765701

MILITARY HISTORY AT YOUR FINGERTIPS
www.naval-military-press.com
ONLINE GENEALOGY RESEARCH
www.military-genealogy.com
ONLINE MILITARY CARTOGRAPHY
www.militarymaproom.com

IMPORTANT NOTICE.

I. The first duty of every officer of the Anti-Aircraft Corps is to make himself thoroughly acquainted with the contents of this book. *Officers should clearly understand that every order contained herein is to be carried out.*

II. The contents of this book being highly confidential, its misuse will entail the most serious consequences. Loss should be immediately reported by telephone.

III. Additional orders, which may be issued from time to time, are to be entered in the spaces provided, and the paragraph to which they refer marked.

F. C. HALAHAN,
Commander, R.N.,
Anti-Aircraft Section.

December 31st, 1914.

INDEX.

CHAPTER I.

CHAPTER II.

Notes on Gunnery and Control.

CHAPTER III.

Gun Drill.

CHAPTER IV.

Notes on Searchlights.

u (12)26597 Wt 3958—P 34 100 2/15 E & S

CHAPTER V.

Notes on Musketry and Discipline.

CHAPTER VI.

Control Telephone System.

CHAPTER VII.

CHAPTER VIII.

CHAPTER I.

GENERAL ORGANISATION OF THE ANTI-AIRCRAFT DEFENCES.

I.—GENERAL INFORMATION.

I. The air defence of London and various other large towns is undertaken by the Royal Naval Air Service, of which Captain Murray F. Sueter, C.B., R.N., is director.

II. The Anti-Aircraft Section of the Royal Naval Air Service (Commander F. C. Halahan, R.N., M.V.O., in charge) deals with all questions concerning the lighting of towns, and the establishment of Anti-Aircraft Defences at places not defended by the Military Authorities. It is also responsible for the training of the Anti-Aircraft Corps.

III. The Anti-Aircraft Corps (Captain L. S. Stansfeld, R.N., Inspecting Captain) is established in various towns where the Anti-Aircraft Section have considered it necessary to raise volunteers to man the guns and lights.

IV. The London Division Anti-Aircraft Corps (Commander Grenville G. Grey, R.N.V.R., in command) is responsible for manning certain gun and searchlight stations in London and on the Continent under the surveillance of the Anti-Aircraft Section.

V. All administrative matters concerning the London section of the Anti-Aircraft Corps are dealt with in Room 10, Block IV. (South) Admiralty, by Commander Grey, R.N.V.R.

VI. All matters concerning other sections of the Anti-Aircraft Corps are dealt with in Room 10, Block IV. (South), by Captain Stansfeld.

VII. All matters concerning constructive work at stations, Naval Ratings employed with Anti-Aircraft Corps, lighting, police, &c., are dealt with in Anti-Aircraft Office, Top Floor, Block IV. (South). These matters are dealt with as follows:—

(a) *Commander Halahan* deals with every important matter eventually, but as far as possible nothing but the most urgent business should be taken to him direct.

(b) *Lieutenant-Commander Hincks* deals with all constructive work, and with the provision and upkeep of stores, &c., at stations. Watch-keeping Officer.

(c) *Major Lucas* is in command of the Eastern Counties Mobile Anti-Aircraft Defence. Headquarters, Newmarket.

(d) *Lieutenant Pink* deals with all telephone and alarm bell circuits, inventions, suggestions, and general matters connected with the efficiency of the Anti-Aircraft Defences. Drill Instructor. Watch-keeping Officer.

(e) *Lieutenant Sinclair, R.N.V.R.*, acts as Gunnery Officer and as instructor in signalling. Watch-keeping Officer.

(*f*) *Lieutenant Perrin, R.N.V.R.*, assists in general organisation work and as musketry instructor. Watch-keeping Officer.

VIII. All matters concerning the internal economy of the London Division are dealt with as follows:—

(*a*) Captain Stansfeld is the final authority on all administrative matters connected with the Anti-Aircraft Corps.

(*b*) Commander Grey deals with all important matters affecting the London Division.

(*c*) Lieutenant Hague Cook deals with all transfers, vacancies, substitutes in London Division, and forwards lists of alterations to the Anti-Aircraft Corps Filing Office.

(*d*) Sub-Lieutenant Bennett is in charge of the Filing Office.

(*e*) Assistant-Paymaster Upham deals with all matters affecting pay, discharges, resignations, and passes.

(*f*) Chief Petty Officer Gapp deals with all questions of uniforms.

II.—THE CONTROL SYSTEM.

I. The London Air Defence is divided into a series of units, known as Sub-Controls, acting under the authority of a Central Control.

II. Each of these Sub-Controls consists of one or more guns, and one or more searchlight positions, placed conveniently to act in co-operation.

III. A suitable gun position has been selected in each of these Sub-Controls, which is known as the *Sub-Control Station.* From this station the gun and light positions of the Sub-Control will be directed and controlled.

IV. The Central Control is situated on Admiralty Arch, and is in direct telephonic communication with all Sub-Control Stations and through them with every position in the London defence.

V. The duty Central Control Officer is an officer of the Anti-Aircraft Office, who during his period of duty is in charge of the Anti-Aircraft defence of London. All Sub-Controls are entirely under his orders.

III.—ORDERS FOR OFFICERS.

I. The complement of commissioned officers in the Anti-Aircraft Corps allows for one officer at each gun or searchlight position. Thus there are 2, 3 or 4 officers in each Sub-Control according to the number of attached stations.

II. The senior of these officers in each Sub-Control is known as the Commanding Officer of the Sub-Control (thus: "Commanding Officer Gresham Sub-Control," &c.), and, acting under the supreme authority of Central Control, he is the executive and administrative head of his Sub-Control.

III. The duties of all officers in charge of guns and searchlights are threefold:—

(*a*) Administrative work in connection with their stations and its crew.

(*b*) The maintenance of their respective guns or lights, and their stations generally in efficient condition.

(*c*) Watch-keeping duty at their Sub-Control Station.

As regards (*a*). They are responsible that every watch at their station is efficient in its duties, and that in the case of absentees, substitutes are provided. They are to forward all applications for leave of absence, reports of sickness, &c. to their respective Commanding Officers, who will bring or forward them to Headquarters. When time presses reports may be forwarded by telephone.

They will also forward a regular "daily report" to their Commanding Officer of all duties, drills, &c. carried out at their station, and all requisitions for stores, &c. (The Commanding Officer will attach such portions of these reports as he considers necessary to his own "daily report.")

As regards (*b*). Applications of technical assistance at guns or searchlights must be forwarded to Headquarters through the Commanding Officers of Sub-Controls. Breakages or failure of instruments should always be reported *immediately* by telephone.

As regards (*c*). The Commanding Officer of each Sub-Control is to arrange the watches on the following lines:—

(1) The Central and all Sub-Control Stations are always to have an officer on duty, and are never to be left without one under any circumstances. From 10 p.m. to 8 a.m. there is to be an officer at every gun station.

(2) If officers require meals whilst on duty, they must make arrangements for them to be supplied at their stations.

(3) If at any time the Commanding Officer of the Corps requires an officer who is on duty at Headquarters or elsewhere, for any special reason, another officer must be sent to relieve him, but an officer on duty is not to be sent for except by the Commanding Officer or the Duty Central Control Officer.

(4) Conversations over the telephone with regard to duty often lead to misunderstandings and should only be resorted to in cases of necessity.

(5) When officers for their own convenience arrange to undertake long hours of duty, these orders are not to be relaxed in any manner.

In any case an officer off duty must never be out of touch with the telephone, and must leave his telephone number with the Duty Sub-Control Officer of his Sub-Control.

IV. The duties of the Duty Sub-Control Officer are as follows:—

(A) In case of attack he will be entirely responsible for the efficient co-operation of his guns and lights, and for the carrying out of the various instructions issued by Central Control.

(B) He will be ready both by day and night to take instant action in the case of emergency.

(C) He will frequently visit the gun platform of his Sub-Control Station and exercise the guns' crews.

(D) He will frequently exercise his gun's crew in Rifle exercises and Squad drill.

(E) He will keep in constant telephonic touch with the gun and light positions in his Sub-Control, assuring himself frequently as to their efficiency and readiness.

(F) He will frequently examine his telephone operators as to their knowledge of the switchboard and will exercise them by obtaining calls along the "loop line," carrying out the routine of an "alarm," &c.

(G) He will cause all the stations in his Sub-Control to report their watch correct or otherwise at every relief, and having received all reports he will inform Central Control.

(H) He will never leave his station until properly relieved, unless he has received express permission from Central Control to do so.

V. *As far as possible officers not on duty as Duty Sub-*Control Officers are expected to be present at evening quarters. The Commanding Officer of each Sub-Control will arrange at what positions in the Sub-Control he wishes the officers to be.

VI. The duties of Commanding Officers of Sub-Controls are as follows:—

(A) They are entirely responsible for the efficiency and good order of their Sub-Controls.

(B) They will personally investigate all cases of alleged misconduct before reporting the matter to Headquarters. Reports should, as a rule, be made clearly in writing and forwarded with the daily report.

(C) In a case where instant action is required, however, the Commanding Officer or Duty Sub-Control Officer (if Commanding Officer is absent) should act on his own initiative and report to Headquarters by telephone.

(D) No Commanding Officer has the right to inflict any punishment whatsoever.

(E) They will frequently inspect the Positions in their Sub-Controls, and exercise the officers and crews in gun drill, rifle exercises, squad drill, &c. They will also note and remark upon the cleanliness, efficiency and good order of the stations, adding this to their "daily report."

(F) They are to pay special attention to the training of their officers and give them every opportunity of becoming thoroughly conversant with the construction, working and method of drilling at their guns and lights.

VII. All officers are expected to perfect themselves in the drill and manipulation of the guns, lights, rifles and pistols in order that at any time they may correct faults and instruct their subordinates in their various duties. Officers must remember that they cannot consider themselves efficient until they possess more practical and theoretical technical knowledge than any man (Naval Ratings or Anti-Aircraft Corps) employed at any gun or light position in their Sub-Control.

VIII. All officers should take every opportunity of setting clearly before their subordinates the general lines on which the Anti-Aircraft Defence is worked, in order that they may understand the reason for everything which is done.

NOTES.

Maintenance of Stations.—All reports of defects, requirements, &c., &c., should be sent in by each station in the daily report to the Sub-Control Officer and he should satisfy himself that they are genuine and necessary; if breakages they should be investigated by him as to whether due to carelessness or not. Defects affecting the working efficiency of guns or lights at the stations should be reported by telephone at once if necessary to save time and also sent in in writing.

Conditions at Stations.—Stations are of necessity very differently designed owing to the different times when they have been built and the different places where they are situated. Wherever circumstances admit a hut has been provided as a shelter for the men not actually on watch, including those of the R.N.V.R. who live at a distance from the station and who have to keep the middle and morning watches. There is also a telephone hut and, in the case of gun stations, an ammunition shed. A separate room for the accommodation of the Naval Ratings is also provided.

At gun stations where an Officer has to sleep at the gun a small room is provided for him to sleep in.

IV.—EXTRACT OF GENERAL ORDERS FOR ALL STATIONS.

I. Every C.P.O. and man at the Sub-Control Station should be prepared at a moment's notice to undertake *any* duty at the station, including that of Sub-Control Officer and Telephone Operator.

NOTE WELL.—In the case of a breakdown, an accident, or the station being sniped, they may actually have to rely entirely upon their own resources. Officers of stations should, therefore, afford their men every opportunity of learning how to perform any and every duty at the stations.

II. *At Gun Stations.*—In case of sudden alarm the Senior Naval Petty Officer will take the Officer's position until the arrival of the Officer himself. He will carry out the instructions received from Central and act generally as Officer until relieved. (The Second Senior Naval Rating will take No. 1 at the gun.)

At Light Stations the Anti-Aircraft Corps Chief P.O. will take charge in the same way.

III. The Sub-Control Officers will always be prepared to explain to their men the orders and methods used in Anti-Aircraft Defence, and if any improvements or alterations are suggested, they will always receive consideration.

IV. Men should be thoroughly acquainted with the names and appearance of all Officers of the Anti-Aircraft Section and of the Anti-Aircraft Corps.

V. *Sick List.*—When men are absent from duty owing to sickness, they should report immediately by telephone or telegraph to the Commanding Officer of their Sub-Control. If absent for more than one watch, medical certificate must be obtained and forwarded to Headquarters.

VI. *Leave.*—Officers Commanding Stations can grant leave off a "watch," provided a substitute is found and all duties properly carried on. Only on application to Headquarters can leave be granted for 48 hours or more.

VII. If men wish to write on Service matters to their Commanding Officer (*i.e.*, to report sick, request leave, &c.), they should address him thus :—

The Commanding Officer,

(*Name of Sub-Control*) ________________

(*Full Postal Address of Sub-Control Station*) ________________ ________________

NOTE I.—In case of actually seeing and hearing an aircraft in the immediate vicinity of the Sub-Control, the Senior Rating present should immediately order the alarm to be sounded to all stations in the Sub-Control and inform

Central. He should not waste time in discussing the matter, but should act on his own initiative at once.

NOTE II.—ON THE "ALARM" SOUNDING AT ANY TIME, THE GUNS AND LIGHTS CREWS WILL IMMEDIATELY CLOSE UP AND PREPARE FOR INSTANT ACTION, BUT NO GUNS ARE TO BE ACTUALLY LOADED OR LIGHTS SWITCHED ON UNTIL THE RECEIPT OF DEFINITE ORDERS TO DO SO.

V.—ORDERS FOR NAVAL RATINGS AT ALL GUN STATIONS MANNED BY ANTI-AIRCRAFT CORPS.

1. Chief P.O.s and P.O.1. rank senior to Anti-Aircraft Corps Chief P.O.s. All other ratings rank junior to Anti-Aircraft C.P.O., but senior to R.N.V.R. A.B.s.

2. In the absence of a commissioned officer, the Senior Naval Rating will always take charge in case of alarm, and assume the officer's position until relieved by a commissioned officer.

3. The primary duty of the Naval Ratings is to impart instructions to the Anti-Aircraft Ratings, and to keep the gun, station fittings, &c., in efficient and clean condition.

4. The Naval Ratings are to be divided into two divisions of equal numbers. The two divisions will be on duty alternately—working in 24-hour spells.

5. The Duty Division will in turn be divided into two watches, one watch being always on duty either on the gun platform or its immediate vicinity, and the other resting below. The watch on duty are expected to give instructions whenever required during their watch, but at the same time

they are not to lose sight of the fact that an important part of their duty is to keep good look-out.

6. Divisions are permitted to proceed on leave at the end of their period of duty, but none of the division are to leave the station until properly relieved and after all orders have been turned over in the proper Service manner.

7. No exchanges of duty will be permitted between members of the Duty and Non-Duty Divisions unless application has been made the previous day through the Chief G.M. at the Admiralty. In any case no member of the Duty Division is ever to leave the station unless express permission has been received from the Duty Central Control Officer, Admiralty, and a relief has been provided. This permission will never be granted except in urgent cases.

8. No provision is made for members of the Non-Duty Division sleeping at their stations. They are never to do so except by express permission of the Commander. Lodging and compensation is paid to cover this outlay.

9. On the alarm being sounded at any time, whether for exercise or for any other purpose, *every* rating on the station, whether duty or non-duty, is to immediately proceed to his post of duty and assist as required.

10. All ratings are warned that they hold very responsible positions while employed on the Anti-Aircraft Defence of London, and that only men whose conduct is above suspicion in every way can be employed upon this important duty. Consequently, *any* misdemeanour on the part of a rating will entail his immediate return to his Depôt.

11. All requests from Naval Ratings are to be forwarded to the Commander through the Chief Gunner's Mate at the Admiralty.

12. Should any case occur of ratings failing to return in time to keep their watch, the matter is to be immediately reported by telephone to the duty C.P.O., Admiralty Arch.

VI.—ORDERS FOR NAVAL RATINGS AT ALL SEARCHLIGHT STATIONS.

1. The primary duty of the Naval Ratings is to impart instructions to the Anti-Aircraft Corps Ratings and keep the lights, station fittings, &c. in efficient and clean condition.

2. There are two Naval Ratings at each station, who will work spells of 24 hours about, relieving at 12 noon daily, or by mutual arrangement.

3. From evening quarters till daylight no exchanges of duty whatever are to take place between the duty and non-duty ratings, except in the case of illness, &c., by permission of the duty sub-control officer, who will immediately inform Central Control.

4. The duty torpedo rating must never leave the station on any account whatever. He is not intended to keep a strict watch, but is to be ready for an immediate call when required. By day he is always to be within hearing of the telephone, unless required by the exigencies of his duties elsewhere. He is always to be on duty at the searchlight at evening quarters and whenever the alarm is sounded, and to act generally as Electrician to the lights.

5. The duty rating is to relieve the Anti-Aircraft Corps crew at official daylight and take over the station in the proper service manner.

6. The non-duty rating has permission to proceed on leave as soon as relieved, but he is never to proceed on leave until he has properly turned over the station and all orders, &c. to his relief.

7. The non-duty rating is *never* to sleep at the light station, except by express permission of the Commander. Lodging and compensation is paid to cover this expense.

8. All requests from Naval Ratings are to be forwarded to the Commander, through the Chief Torpedo Gunner's Mate at the Admiralty.

NOTE.—The Duty Torpedo Rating will never take executive control of the station. He is employed solely as the technical expert.

CHAPTER II.

NOTES ON GUNNERY AND CONTROL.

I.—GUNNERY.

Shoeburyness.—The Corps exists for the sake of the guns, and it is of the first importance that their crews should attain the highest possible efficiency in their working. At present as many men as possible are taken down almost daily to the ranges at Shoeburyness where a 1-pdr. Pom-Pom, and a 3-inch Hotchkiss gun are available for practice. The number of rounds fired by each man is necessarily limited, but the practice should prove most valuable to those attending, and it is expected that not only those actually firing the guns at the moment, but all the others as well will pay the closest attention to every detail of the drill, the jambs as they occur and means of remedying them, the sighting of the gun and the spotting of the shots fired.

Sights.—With regard to the sights fitted to the guns. The graduation of these, which is based upon the assumption that the object is more or less upon the same level as the gun, ceases to be applicable to the actual range when the gun is elevated to the amount probable in case of aircraft attack. Obviously when the gun is vertical no elevation of the sights is required for any range within the power of the gun, and as the object approaches the horizontal the sight scales approach nearer and nearer to the truth. Except for the absolute vertical position, however, some elevation of the sights is necessary, and the figures on the sight scales are useful as enabling some definite order to be given to the sightsetter. In the case of aircraft approaching end on and passing overhead, the surest way of hitting her will be to fire at some point ahead of her and let her come into the stream of fire.

Deflection.—The purpose of the Deflection Scale which has no application to the last-named case is (*a*) to direct the fire sufficiently ahead of a crossing aircraft to allow for her speed and (*b*) to allow for the effect of the wind. In such weather as is likely to admit of the coming of aircraft, the purpose (*a*) is practically the only one to be considered. Deflection is put on in the direction in which the object is proceeding, that is, an object coming from right to left requires left deflection, and *vice versâ*.

Orders for Range.—Ranges are to be called out in full telephone number fashion, except in the even thousands which are to be called as thousands, *e.g.*, one seven double oh—two thousand. ("Ups" and "Downs," as "Up 200," "Down 50" are not to be used.)

Orders for Deflection.—The numbers on the Deflection Scale after the first are not to be given from zero but from the last number, example:—left five being on the scale the order "Right Ten," does not mean ten to the right from zero, but ten to the right from left five, *i.e.*, Right five. If in doubt as to the deflection in the case of a crossing airship, a shot aimed with no deflection at the nose of the airship will at all likely speeds and ranges probably hit amidships or a little aft of the airship.

NOTES.

I. The sight to be taken with a gun sight is exactly the same as that to be taken with a rifle sight, *see* illustration on page 57.

II. In firing at a target, the same spot on the target must always be aimed at, or spotting corrections are useless.

III. If the actual effect of the shot cannot be seen, the "tracers" will indicate its direction and enable the spotter to give directions to the sightsetter. There are two sorts of tracers, "day" and "night." The day tracer consists of a dark fluid enclosed in a cavity in the shell which escapes through a small hole during the flight of the shell producing a smoke effect. The night tracer is a composition ignited by the discharge of the gun, producing a light easily followed by the eye.

IV. In giving directions to the sightsetter it is absolutely essential that they should be given clearly, decisively, and on the instant.

II.—NOTES ON ATTACK.

I. The Duty Sub-Control Officer at each Sub-Control will receive general instructions and information from the Central Control, but is entirely responsible for the actual working of his guns and lights.

II. HE IS NEVER TO OPEN FIRE WITHOUT FIRST RECEIVING PERMISSION TO DO SO FROM THE CENTRAL CONTROL, UNLESS A HOSTILE AIRSHIP OR AEROPLANE ACTUALLY DROPS A BOMB, AND IS LOCATED IN HIS IMMEDIATE VICINITY.

It must not be forgotten, however, that telephone communication may easily be interrupted.

III. A COMPLETE BREAKDOWN OF THE CENTRAL CONTROL COMMUNICATIONS WILL BE SIGNALLED BY THREE WHITE SIGNAL ROCKETS, FIRED AT A FEW SECONDS' INTERVAL FROM THE ADMIRALTY ARCH. Should this signal be seen by any station, it is to be passed on to all Sub-Control Stations, through the "loop lines," and the Duty Sub-Control Officers will assume independent charge of their respective Sub-Controls, acting in the spirit of the general orders until communication is restored.

The above signal (three white rockets) is introduced solely to cover the possibility of the Central Control Station being destroyed by a lucky shot from the enemy, or a successful attack by spies on the telephone system, and will not be made use of in the event of only one or two lines failing, as in the latter event communication with Central can be maintained through the "loop lines."

IV. Each Sub-Control Station is fitted with an alarm bell worked by a push from the Central Control. In addition, each gun or searchlight position is fitted with an alarm bell, worked by a push from its Sub-Control Station. These alarm bell circuits are quite independent of the telephone circuits, and their ringing cannot possibly be mistaken for one of the telephones.

On hearing this bell at any station, the gun or lights crew should immediately "close up," and make all preparations for instant action.

The "Alarm" with any possible information and orders will immediately afterwards be confirmed by telephone from Central to Sub-Controls and from Sub-Controls to their stations.

V. If an airship is sighted by one of the stations in a Sub-Control or by a Sub-Control Station itself, the Sub-Control Officer should immediately ring the alarm to all his stations, at the same time informing the Central Control.

He should then bring his guns and lights to the "*Ready*" and await further orders, in the meantime gaining all possible information as regards the airship or aeroplane and passing same to the Central Control. HE IS NOT TO OPEN FIRE WITHOUT FIRST RECEIVING PERMISSION UNLESS THE AIRSHIP COMMITS AN HOSTILE ACT.

"PERMISSION TO OPEN FIRE" FROM CENTRAL CONTROL IS NOT AN EXECUTIVE ORDER TO BLAZE AWAY INDISCRIMINATELY. IT ONLY MEANS THAT THE SUB-CONTROL OFFICER HAS PERMISSION TO OPEN FIRE OR SWITCH ON HIS LIGHTS WHEN HE CONSIDERS THE AIRSHIP IS SUFFICIENTLY WITHIN RANGE TO WARRANT HIS ATTACKING HER. HE SHOULD REMEMBER THAT IT IS ALWAYS BETTER TO WITHHOLD FIRE UNLESS HE CONSIDERS THERE IS A REASONABLE CHANCE OF HITTING THE OBJECT, FULLY REALISING THAT EVERY PROJECTILE FIRED WILL FINALLY FALL IN A THICKLY POPULATED CITY.

VI. The Sub-Control Officer should remember that if the airship can be clearly seen over the gun sights (for instance, on a bright moonlight night), it is far better not to switch on his lights at all. In other words, the searchlight is merely an aid to the gunlayers and serves no other purpose. If, however, he needs additional light, he should again remember that one searchlight well on the target will be of more use than two or three badly worked, and, in addition, by only having one light he is not giving away his position as two or three lights might do.

III.—EVENING QUARTERS.

(*a*) Evening quarters is a daily exercise intended to accustom officers to control the co-operation of their guns and lights, and to teach guns and lights crews to carry out orders received by telephone as they would have to do in the case of actual attack.

(*b*) The time of evening quarters will be forwarded weekly to all stations by the Commanding Officer A.A.C.

(*c*) The executive order for evening quarters will be a 10-sec. ring on the alarm bell, confirmed over the telephone as "Alarm for quarters."

(*d*) On the alarm bell ringing, the telephone operator will carry out the usual "alarm" orders, and the guns and lights crews will "close up" and prepare as in the case of ordinary attack.

(*e*) As soon as the Duty Sub-Control Officers are satisfied that their respective sub-controls are ready for action they will report to central control "............ Sub-control ready."

(*f*) Exercises will then be carried out as ordered by Central Control.

(*g*) On the completion of the exercises Central Control will give the order to "Secure and call the watch," and will at the same time pass the range for the night. Guns will then be left cleared away, but may be covered. (Before covering the range given will be put on all sights.) Spare ammunition will be covered up, &c., and the ordinary watch will be resumed. Searchlights will be left absolutely ready for use, but may be covered and the ordinary watch will be resumed.

(*h*) As soon as the Duty Sub-Control Officers are satisfied that their respective Sub-Controls are properly secured, they will report to Central Control "............. Sub-control Secured."

NOTE.—The only targets available at quarters are, as a general rule, the beams of other searchlights. This is not satisfactory, but the best that can be done. During quarters, too, is the only time when the searchlights' crews can practice with their lights. Consequently, on receiving an order to attack any given light, all searchlights in the Sub-Control should be used (as opposed to what would be done in the case of actual attack), and superimposed on the highest point of the beam indicated. Guns should also be kept trained on the point of the beam and "action" exercised. Officers should give frequent alterations of range and deflection as the target beam moves through the sky. This is good practice both for the officers themselves and for the sightsetters.

IV.—AMMUNITION.

THE FOLLOWING RULES CONCERNING THE PRESERVATION OF AMMUNITION FOR ANTI-AIRCRAFT GUNS ARE TO BE ADHERED TO.

(*a*) *6-pdr. Cartridges.*—Great care should be taken in handling these cartridges, and the clips should not be removed from the base of the cartridges until immediately before entering the cartridge in the gun for service. Great care should be taken not to drop or knock these cartridges, as a small dent is liable to cause them to jamb. All lids of boxes should be examined and tried to ensure they open readily in case of necessity, but the cartridge boxes should not be opened for any other purpose.

(*b*) *Pom-Pom Shells with Nose Fuses.*—The greatest care in handling these cartridges is required. They should never be allowed to knock or fall on the deck, as a very small burr on the cartridge will cause a bad jamb. The fuses also are very sensitive.

(*c*) *Shell with Nose Fuses* (*Time and Percussion*) *and also Fixed Ammunition.*—When such ammunition is unboxed, it should be placed in bins or raised off the floor by battens. The fuse could not be set to the required length and kept so set so as to be ready to be loaded into the gun in the shortest possible time on an alarm being given. The time pin of this fuse should only be removed immediately before entering the projectile in the gun. These projectiles should never be placed in the gun except for actual service in the case of a known attack being imminent. The pins once removed cannot be replaced.

General.—All ammunition kept out in the open wherever possible should be stood on battens and covered with tarpaulins.

CHAPTER III.

GUN-DRILL.

I.—DRILL FOR "POM-POM" GUNS.

The crew consists of 4 men (3 men and one sightsetter).

Quick Time.	Procedure.
CLOSE UP.	1. The G.L. on left of gun. 2. The loader on right of gun. (Sightsetter on left of gun.) 3. In rear of two.
ACTION.	G.L. sees the elevating and training gear clear. 2 raises the cover, examines and tries the mechanism, removes the lock. G.L. looks through barrel, and, if clear, reports "BORE CLEAR." 2 replaces the lock, puts down the cover. G.L. eases the spring of the lock. 2 fills the barrel casing and buffer provides and places a belt. 3 supplies filled belts. Sightsetter examines sights, if correct, reports "SIGHTS CORRECT."

NOTE.—This is termed the "CLEARED AWAY" position.

Quick Time.	Procedure.
OBJECT.	G.L. trains and lays the gun for the object, and see indicator to "SAFE." 2 passes the end of the belt through the feed block from right to left and sightsetter seizes it. 2 loads the gun by pushing the crank-handle forward. Sightsetter pulls belt to the left as far as it will go. 2 releases crank-handle and then repeats the operation.

NOTE I.—On each occasion the belt must not be pulled before the crank-handle is forward, nor while the crank-handle is going back. The crank-handle must be released and allowed to fly back, on no account must it be eased back. Inattention to these points causesmany jambs.

NOTE II.—This is termed the "GUN-LOADED" position.

DISTANCE	Sightsetter adjusts the sights and reports "SIGHTS SET." This is termed the "READY" position, *i.e.* gun in every respect ready to fire.

NOTE.—Whilst loading, the indicator must be at "SAFE."

INDEPENDENT.	G.L. puts the safety lever to "AUTOMATIC" and then opens fire by pressing the firing key in the training handle. After a burst of about five rounds he will discontinue the fire, the sight will be adjusted to correct the fall of shot and the firing is continued.

Quick Time.	Procedure.
CHECK.	G.L. discontinues the firing.
COMMENCE.	As for independent.
CEASE FIRE.	G.L. discontinues the firing and puts indicator to "SAFE." 2 then raises the cover, removes lock, takes out filled cartridges and passes them to 3, who puts them in a place of safety. Then removes empty cylinders from ejector tube, replaces locks and secures cover. G.L. eases the spring of the lock. 2 withdraws the belt and makes it up. 3 returns the full belts.

NOTE.—It is left to the discretion of the senior officer or rating present whether the gun is left in the "CLEARED AWAY or "GUN LOADED" position.

SECURE.	All numbers replace the gear which they cleared away and leave the gun empty, lock eased, the boxes of ammunition closed. Sightsetter puts sights to zero.

In trying the mechanism when the cover is up, the crank-handle is to be eased back, as the buffer block is not in place in order to prevent damage to the extractor.

MISSFIRES.

If a missfire occurs in rapid or single shot firing G.L. reports "STILL MISSFIRE, CARRY ON." To re-load in this case the crank-handle must be turned forward, the

Quick Time.	Procedure.
	belt pulled to the left, and the crank-handle released; firing can then be continued.
MISSFIRES.	If second missfire occurs G.L. puts safety lever to "SAFE" and orders shift lock. 2 raises lock, removes cartridges and shifts lock. 3 provides spare lock. Gun is then reloaded. If any difficulty occurs in moving the crank-handle, the cover must be raised and the cause ascertained and corrected. To shift a lock, raise the cover, turn the crank-handle forward, lift the fore part of the lock and ease the crank-handle to the rear again; the lock is attached to the connecting rod of the crank by an interrupted thread, one-eighth of a turn to the left releases it from it. The new lock is placed in the reverse order.
	Jambs that may occur and how to remedy them:— In belts loaded by hand, a common cause of a jamb is a badly-loaded belt, the belt being unable to pass through the feed block, when this is observed the belt must be removed and corrected. Accidental stoppages in the automatic action of the gun are due to several other causes, the most likely of which are given below.

Quick Time.	Procedure.
	As the position of the crank-handle will generally indicate to what cause a jamb is due, its position should be carefully observed directly a stoppage occurs.

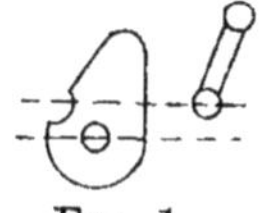

FIG. 1.

(*a*) The lock cannot come back far enough to allow the extractor to drop; or

(*b*) Extractor has dropped but lock still back the length of the cartridge.

JAMBS.

Cause (*a*).—Too heavy tension on fusee spring, want of lubrication, or a light charge.

Remedy.—Throw crank-handle forward and let go. Gun is then ready to fire. If stoppage is repeated ease up fusee spring.

Cause (*b*).—Cartridge canted in lock.

Remedy.—Work crank-handle. If it occurs again shift lock, as it is due probably to a weak gib spring.

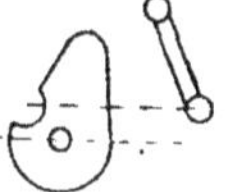

FIG. 2.

Lock can not go right forward after recoil.

Quick Time. | Procedure.

Cause.—Base of cartridge torn off and case left in the chamber.

Remedy.—Remove lock and then remove empty cylinder by the clearing plug.

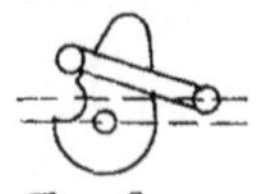

Extractor unable to rise to its highest position although lock is almost home.

FIG. 3.

Cause.—Too light tension on fusee spring or fault in feed.

Remedy.—Strike crank-handle sharply with right hand to send it home. If it occurs again, increase tension on fusee spring. If fusee spring is at maximum tension, lubricate all working parts.

If crank-handle cannot be easily sent home by a blow, it is probably due to cartridge not being exactly in line with groove of extraction, and cover must then be raised and extractor forced down by screwdriver.

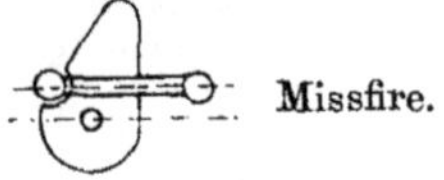

Missfire.

FIG. 4.

Remedy.

Go through loading motions.

If missfire is repeated, raise the cover, and if extractor is right down, the

Quick Time.	Procedure.
	side or extractor levers are broken, and lock must be shifted. If extractor is up in place, lock spring probably weak or firing pin worn or broken. The crank-handle should never be worked when the lock is removed from the gun, as the interrupted thread on the connecting rod is liable to be burred by striking the trigger bar. To clear the ejector tube take out the empty cylinder by hand.

PREPARATION FOR ACTION.

TO FILL WATER JACKET.	1. Lay gun horizontal, see that emptying-plug is home, and fill through filling-hole till it overflows. (It holds about 12 pints.)
TO FILL THE BUFFER.	2. Lay gun horizontal and fill through filling-hole until it overflows. (About 1½ pints mixed water and glycerine.) Replace the plug.
BORE CLEAR.	3. Bore to be seen clear when lock is being examined from muzzle end.
EXAMINE WORKING PARTS OF GUN.	4. Replace the lock and hang the lock on the cam-pawls. Pull the barrel back two or three times and examine and oil the barrel front and rear. Also oil both recoil plates, cams, lock guides, crank bearing and the cover of guide block. Replace feed and secure cover.

Quick Time,	Procedure.
Test Crank Spring.	5 Test with a spring balance— Minimum = 30 lbs. Maximum = 36 lbs. Adjust if necessary ¼ turn of adjustment = 4 to 6 lbs.

NOTES ON DRILL.

Drill.	Position of " Close up."
Single Shot Firing.	Indicator should be put to " Single " or " Auto " according to type of fire required.
Tracers.	Are to be fitted to the first two sheels of each belt, and to every 5th sheel as well.
Firing and Loading.	Gunlayer should fire five rounds at a time and see the effect of his shots. Corrections will be given to the S.S., who will call " On." The G.L. will then fire another burst of five, and so on. When the belt is finished No. 3, assisted by No. 2, if necessary, will insert a new belt as soon as the old one is clear. If the gun stops firing, 1 puts the indicator to " safe," orders " still," and reports " Missfire." The most likely cause of missfire is an expended belt. Jams should never be examined or corrected unless the indicator is at " Safe." In the event of the lock being damaged it is shifted by 2 and 3.

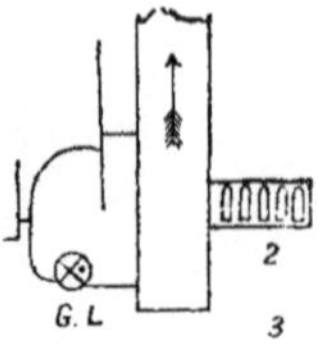

G. L
2
3

II.—DRILL FOR 3-PDR. AND 6-PDR. HOTCHKISS GUN.

The Gun's Crew consists of G.L., Sightsetter, and two Loaders.

Quick Time.	Procedure.
Close up.	1 the G.L. at the shoulder piece. 2 the breech worker on the right in line with the breech. 3 the loader on the left in line with the breech. S.S. at the sights.
Action.	G.L. and 2 clear away all obstructions in the way of working the gun. G.L. eases up the training and elevating clamps. Trains clear and sets them up again. 2 opens the breech. G.L. looks through the bore, and if clear, reports to the Officer " Gun bore clear."

NOTE.—When a gun has been left in the "cleared away" position, on all subsequent occasions of the gun's crew closing up, the Officer is to receive the same report from G.L. before giving the order to "load."

2 eases the spring so that G.L. can see the point of the firing pin, and examines the extractor, and closes the breech.

S.S. works his sight through full limits of elevation and deflection.

3 provides box full of ammunition, and places it on the left of the gun and the gun's crew close up.

The gun is now in the "cleared away" position.

Quick Time.	Procedure.
Bearing and object with its distinctive features.	S.S. repeats all bearings passed and sees deflection scale to zero. G.L. eases up the training and elevating clamps and trains the gun to the named bearing. 2 opens the breech. 3 removes the clip from, and enters the cartridge half-way.

NOTE.—This is termed the "gun loaded" position, *i.e.*, gun loaded, but the breech open.

Range and deflection.	S.S. adjusts the sights.
Independent.	S.S. repeats the order. 3 forces home the cartridge. 2 closes the breech and reports "Ready." G.L. places his finger on the trigger. S.S. reports his sight set. 3 takes another cartridge from the box and removes the clip. This is termed the "ready position," *i.e.*, gun in every respect ready to fire. G.L. fires at his own discretion, bearing in mind that rapidity of fire is essential. When the gun has fired, 2 opens the breech and the loading is carried out as before, and the firing continued.
Common.	3 passes the order to hand up, removes both pins from fuse before inserting the cartridge in the gun and reports "Pins out."

NOTE.—The firing is continued with the shell available until the named shell are passed up.

Quick Time.	Procedure.
Check.	S.S. repeats the order and keeps his sight set. G.L. discontinues the fire and removes his finger from the trigger and orders "Half Cock." 2 opens the breech carefully and leaves the gun in the "Gun loaded" position. G.L. rests his eye but keeps the gun roughly laid and trained on the object.
Half-cock.	As for "Check."

NOTE.—If the gun has just been fired, 3 takes another cartridge from the box, removes the clip, and holds it with the projectile resting on the breech.

Independent.	3 forces home cartridge. 2 closes the breech and reports "Ready." G.L. seizes pistol grip or lever, and the firing is continued.
Re-cock.	2 re-cocks with the re-cocking handle, places his hand on the gun and reports "Ready" and the firing is continued.
Shift Hammer.	2 eases the spring (if the hammer is cocked), inserts the point of the screw driver into the seat of the main spring, compresses it, slips the arms of the stirrup off its end, and removes the main spring; turns the stirrup to a horizontal position so as to unlock the rocking shaft, pulls out the rocking shaft and removes the hammer. 3 provides a spare hammer. 2 inserts the spare hammer, carrying out the above procedure in the reverse order, places

Quick Time.	Procedure.
	his hand on the gun, and reports "Ready." G.L. seizes the pistol grip, and the firing is continued.
Cease firing.	S.S. repeats the order. G.L. discontinues the firing, and removes his finger from the trigger. 2 opens the breech carefully. 3 returns the cartridge in hand, and receives the one from the gun, returns it to the box. 2 closes the breech and the gun's crew close up.

NOTE.—(*a*) It is left to the discretion of the Officer whether the gun is left in the "Gun loaded" or "Cleared away" position.

(*b*) Care has to he taken that any cartridge which has been entered in the gun and subsequently withdrawn, is kept separate from cartridges which have not been entered.

(*c*) Cartridges which have been passed up, but which have not entered in the gun—

If undamaged, are to be returned to the magazine after the Officer has inspected them.

If damaged, to be returned in separate cases from those containing undamaged charges, and returned to the Admiralty at the first opportunity.

Cartridges that have been entered in the gun, unless there is an opportunity of using them up during the practice then in progress, are to be dealt with as follows:—

If the gun has been heated by the firing, the cartridge complete is to be removed to a place of safety. No attempt is to be made to remove the charge from the cylinder.

If withdrawn from a cold gun, no special precautions are necessary, and the cartridges should be treated as if they had not been entered in the gun.

Quick Time.	Procedure.
Secure.	G.L. sets up elevating and training clamps. S.S. runs the sight to zero. 3 returns the ammunition boxes. All numbers replace gear which they cleared away. When finished, G.C. to reports O.O.Q., " — gun secured," falls the gun's crew out, and stands them at ease.

Missfires.

G.L. removes his hand from the pistol grip or firing lever, orders "Still," reports "Missfire" and then orders "Re-cock."

2 sees that the crank handle is properly closed and then re-cocks by means of the re-cocking lever, and reports "Ready."

G.L. seizes the pistol grip or firing grip and the firing is continued. If the gun fails to fire a second time, G.L. again orders "Still" and reports to Officer.

The Officer waits a pause of 15 minutes (to be measured by a watch) and then orders "Shift cartridge."

2 opens the breech carefully.

3 removes the cartridge, if the cap has been struck, the cartridge is to be placed in a safe spot, and a new one inserted. If not struck a new hammer complete is to be put into the gun.

NOTE.—(*a*) When waiting the pause of 15 minutes, if the crew are fallen out, a sentry is to be posted at the gun, whose sole duty is to keep the gun laid in the safest direction, and to prevent anybody interfering with the breech mechanism.

(*b*) When the missfires occur at these guns, the practice is to be suspended until the breech mechanism has been examined, the following points being noted :—

(1) The state of the notch for "Catch retaining lever forward."

(2) The looseness or otherwise of the crank axle on its bearing.

(3) The position of the crank handle when the missfire occurred.

(*c*) Full particulars are to be reported immediately to central in the case of a missfired cartridge being found struck.

III.—DRILL FOR 3-INCH ANTI-AIRCRAFT SEMI-AUTOMATIC GUNS.

The Gun's crew consists of Gunlayer, Trainer, two Sight-setters, Breech Worker, Loader, and one ammunition number.

NOTE.—One additional fusesetter is required for rapid firing.

Quick Time.	Procedure.
QUICK TIME. CLOSE UP.	G.L. at elevating handle on left seat. 4 Trainer at training handle on right seat. S.S. in line with the sights. 2 on the right in line with the breech clear of the recoil. 3 on left in line with the breech. 5 in rear of 3. Additional fusesetter in rear of 5.
ACTION.	All numbers clear away obstructions in the way of working the gun. G.L. and 4 provide and ship telescopes and focus them, adjust head rests, seats, and foot rests to positions which suit, as far as possible, all angles of elevation and test elevating and training gear. Sightsetters run their sights to full limit of elevation and deflection. 3 sees pawl locking lever to H. 2 opens breech and places tray of stores in a convenient position.

Quick Time.	Procedure.
	G.L. reports bore clear. 3 provides dummy cartridge for testing firing gear. 5 provides ammunition and fuses shell as ordered.
LOAD.	Officer in charge of gun names fuse-setting of first round to be used. 5 hands a round to 3 who reports "Pins out," and inserts it in the gun, pressing it home with the right hand, first seeing the safety lever to "Safe." 2 closes the breech.

NOTE 2.—The gun is never to be loaded with shell except by direct orders from Admiralty Control, or by orders from the officer in charge of the gun, after airship has committed some hostile act.

BEARING ON OBJECT WITH DISTINCTIVE FEATURES.	G.L. and 4 train on the bearing named. G.L. altering elevating gear from slow to fast if necessary. This is termed the half-cock position, *i.e.*, breech closed, gun loaded safety lever to "Safe," and gun laid.
RANGE AND DEFLECTION SEMI-AUTO.	Sightsetters adjust the sights. 3 sees pawl locking lever to "S.A."
CONTROL OR STAND BY.	3 sees the "safety lever" to "Fire." 2 places his hand on the gun and reports "Ready." G.L. places his hand on the firing lever. S.S.'s reports "Sights set."

Quick Time.	Procedure.
	Loaders take up ammunition. This is termed the "Ready position," *i.e.*, gun in every respect ready to fire.
ORDER FIRE.	G.L. fires when his sights are on and releases his grip on firing lever. Loading carried out as before.
INDEPENDENT.	G.L. continues firing independently so long as his sights are on the target.

NOTE.—After order "Fire or Independent."

If the Control Officer or Spotter sees the shots are going under or over the object, he will correct the range as necessary to bring the shots on the object fired at. Each order being carried out by the Sightsetter.

Should the shots be going Right or Left, the Control Officer will order Left or Right 1 or 2 as necessary, each order meaning one or two notches on the speed vernier. The Sightsetter reporting "On" each time he alters his sights.

CHECK OR HALF COCK.	G.L. removes his hand from the firing lever and with 4 keeps the gun roughly laid on the object with the open sight. 3 puts the "safety lever" to "Safe."
FAILURE OF S. AUTO-GEAR.	Control Officer orders "Quick Firing." 3 puts pawl locking-lever to "H" and to safety lever to "Fire." 2 works the breech.
CEASE FIRING.	G.L. discontinues the fire and removed his hand from the firing lever. 2 opens the breech. 3 removes the cartridge and hands it to 5.

NOTE.—It is left to the discretion of the Control Officer whether the gun is brought to the "gun loaded" or "cleared away" position.

Quick Time.	Procedure.
UNSHIP TELESCOPES.	G.L. and 4 unship telescopes, 4 returning them to their boxes.
UNLOAD.	Always carried out in slow time. 3 sees the pawl locking lever to "H."
OPEN THE BREECH.	2 opens the breech. 3 receives cartridge and hands it to 5.

NOTE.—If projectile remains in the gun owing to being loose in the cartridge, permission must be obtained to fire the gun (only nose-fused shell are supplied to these guns).

SECURE.	G.L. and 4 train to securing position, S.S. runs the sights down to 1,000 yards. Gear replaced by numbers who provided it when clearing away. Gun's crew falls out.

MISSFIRES.

Should the gun fail to fire at any time the G.L.'s order "Missfire" will be preceded by the caution "Still" followed by the order "Carry on."

G.L. removes his hand from the firing lever, reports "Missfire" and then orders "Re-cock."

3 re-cocks by pushing re-cocking lever forward.

2 reports "Ready."

Should the gun fail to fire a second time in succession, G.L. reports "Missfire."

3 puts his levers to "Safe" and "H."

Control Officer waits a pause of one minute, then orders "Shift cartridge."

2 opens the breech carefully.

5 receives the missfired round from 3 and reports whether the cap has been struck or not.

2 is to report bore clear before 3 enters the new cartridge.

If struck, the round is to be placed in a safe place clear of the gun.

If cap is not struck, G.L. orders "Shift striker."

2 sees the chamber empty, closes the breech and releases the striker by turning the firing lever.

2 assisted by 3 removes damaged striker and inserts new striker.

2 opens the breech, 3 re-loads, 2 closes the breech.

3 places pawl locking lever to S.A. 2 reports "Ready."

NOTE.—For drill purposes it is inadvisable to release the striker with the gun empty, the probable result being a broken firing pin.

CHAPTER IV.

NOTES ON SEARCHLIGHTS.

I.—OXY-ACETYLENE SEARCHLIGHT BURNER.

First Operation.—Connect the rubber tube from acetylene generator to tap on burner marked (Act).

Connect tube from oxygen cylinder to tap marked (Oxy).

Care should be taken that these tubes are pushed well home, and, should occasion arise, tie them on.

Second Operation.—See that the acetylene generator is working properly (*see* separate instructions), also that the taps of the burner are shut (*see* Diagram No. 2). Open the oxy cylinder valve (half a complete turn is generally sufficient), and regulate the pressure to 10 lbs. per square inch.

Third Operation : Pastille Adjustment.—Pastilles are very fragile and require careful handling. Diagram No. 1 shows the method of fixing. A gentle pressure applied by the milled edge nut will suffice to hold it firmly. Care should be taken to see that the pastille fits close to the back of the holder. The distance of the pastille from the burner nipple should be about $\frac{1}{10}$ of an inch, and the best position about ¼-inch above the lower edge. The diagram is full size and shows these details. Beneath the burner base will be found

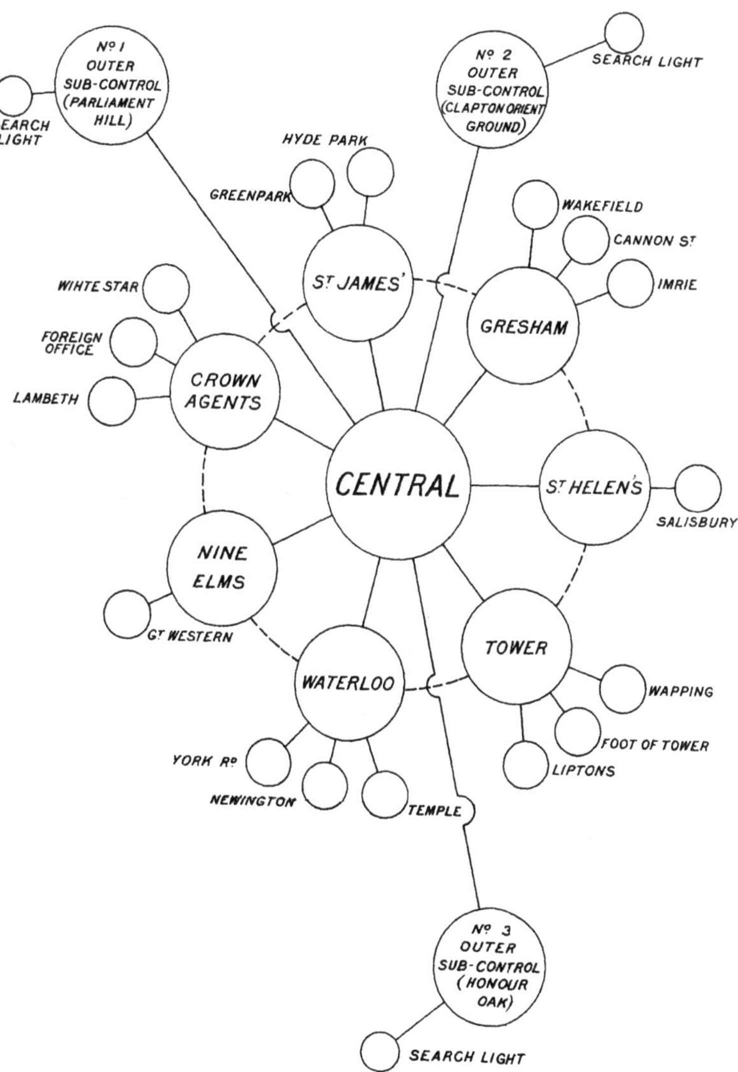

559-39858-P34. 100. 1. 15.

Malby & Sons, Lith.

milled head knobs to operate the pastille as mentioned above.

Fourth Operation: To light the Burner.—Turn on the acetylene at the generator, the oxygen at the reducing valve, and get a lighted taper and apply to the burner below the nipple, and then turn on the burner taps full by pulling the lever slowly as far to the left as it will go (*see* arrow marks). For turning out reverse the lever, also slowly.

General Remarks.—Always turn on and off slowly, as this prevents breakage of the pastilles.

Remember to turn off always at the burner end of the installation. The oxygen and acetylene must always be on at the cylinder and generator end and off at the burner end before attempting to light up.

The burner must be kept clean at the nipples B. on Diagram No. 2 and D. on Diagram No. 1, and also at the gas channel A. Suitable cleaning drills are provided for this purpose, and this should be done about every two weeks.

With ordinary care a pastille will last a week. It does not burn away, but is only blown away in particles by the pressure, or is broken mechanically.

Remember to turn off the oxygen at the cylinder on leaving; turning off the reducing valve is not sufficient.

It sometimes happens that moisture gets into the tubes. Should this happen, allow the taps to remain open for a few seconds before lighting. The presence of moisture is easily detected by the noise and spluttering which takes place at the nipple.

The acetylene generator should be below the burner and the tubes arranged (if possible) to drain away from the burner.

II.—ELECTRIC SEARCHLIGHTS.

To Prepare a Searchlight for Burning.—If there is time, always test the circuits and the adjustment of the lamps beforehand. The greatest care must be taken in fixing the carbons in their holders so that they are perfectly in line both when facing the front and side of the lamp. Unless this is done, the crater will not form evenly, and an unsteady light will be obtained. Never put in a carbon which is not absolutely straight. The carbons should always have the crater and point formed on them beforehand. This can be done by burning them in the daytime, but in the case of horizontal carbons, it can best be done by turning them out in a lathe. The crater should have a depth of three-eighths of the diameter of the carbon; the point should be of one diameter's length.

The gear for adjusting the positive carbon should always be tested to see that it is free enough to enable it to be worked easily, but that it is not so loose that the carbon drops down by its own weight when the set screw is eased up.

The position of the carbons must be adjusted so that the crater is opposite the centre of the mirror when the vertical adjustment of the positive carbon is in its central position. In the inclined lamp this can easily be done by the star wheel, the crater being placed 21¼ inches above the base plate. In the horizontal lamps the negative carbon holder must be clamped at the correct height by careful measurement when in the projector; half-an-inch error is sufficient to spoil the beam.

No rags or gear should be stowed inside the pedestal or in the barrel on account of the danger of fire, and of the liability of their jambing the mechanism.

Always join up the leads and everything ready for burning before it gets dark.

To Burn the Light.—Put the switch in the pedestal to "On" and make any other switches that may be in the circuit. Then close the carbons.

Inclined Hand Lamp.—As soon as the points appear incandescent, separate them slowly and keep them within about a quarter of an inch from one another, as the crater begins to heat. When the carbons are well hot and a crater is beginning to form, separate the carbons to about half an inch and keep them at that distance by closing them in slightly as they burn away. Watch carefully to see if the crater is forming in the lower carbon. If the arc appears beaten down, this probably will occur, and the polarity of the machine is reversed, or the leads are incorrectly joined up. Keep a look-out to see that the crater burns evenly. If any portion of it does not burn away sufficiently, alter the position of the $+^{ve}$ carbon so that the arc will play against that part, taking care to replace the carbon in line as soon as the crater is properly reformed.

The arc, when burning properly, will remain quite silent, but if the carbons are bad ones or the crater is badly formed, the arc will flicker about from one portion of the surface to the other, and a great deal of hissing and flaming will occur. The only cure for this is to close the carbons slightly to heat them up well, and to alter the position of the positive carbon until the crater is reformed. The hissing and bad light will probably be increased whilst this is being done, but it cannot be avoided.

If a button forms on the negative carbon it shows that they have been kept too close together. In this case separate the carbons and chip off the button with a knife, since while the button is there the light will never burn steadily.

With an Automatic Lamp the arc should always be struck by hand, for the automatic gear takes too long to close the carbons in. The instant the carbons touch each other, the series magnet of the lamp will separate them, and it is therefore not necessary to separate them by hand.

Great care must be taken never to work the hand wheel unless the lever is first put to "Hand" (or "Off"), otherwise the pawls will soon be damaged.

When the crater is properly formed, and the arc has become silent, the lamp may be put to burn automatically.

Should the lamp not feed in when it is seen that it should be doing so, do not at once alter the adjustment of the voltage screw, as this adjustment has been carefully made with a voltmeter, and it is very possible it is not the cause of the failure. First work the shunt armature with one finger and see that the pawls are working. Secondly, make sure that the make and break screw is in order. If the armature is heard to be vibrating but no feeling is occurring, there is probably some friction in the gear, or the pawls are at fault. Put lever to hand and work hand wheel to see if the gear is free. A burr on the tooth or a particle of carbon may jamb the mechanism. If "pumping" of the positive carbon occurs, it may be due to any one of the following causes: spring acting against striking coil too strong; striking coil faulty; insufficient current passing through the lamp.

General Remarks on Burning and Management.—Keep the doors of the barrel closed as much as possible whilst burning so as to keep the wind away from the arc.

To put the light out always separate the carbons and so break the arc before breaking away the switch. If a lamp will not burn when in the projector, test for a break with an incandescent lamp between the various points on the mains. If the lamp burns in one position of the projector only, the spring contacts must be at fault.

Always keep the beam carefully focussed; the beam should be as narrow as possible providing that the rays do not cross. If one half of the beam is brighter than the other half it may be due to the bad burning of the crater, or because the crater is not in line with the centre of the mirror.

Allow the projector to cool slowly after use, and do not expose the mirror to a cold draught of air.

CHAPTER V.

NOTES ON MUSKETRY AND DISCIPLINE.

I.—ORDERS FOR SENTRIES.

When posted outdoors :

Sentries will carry their rifle at the slope with fixed bayonets, patrolling their posts in a smart and brisk manner, or if standing still will remain correctly at ease.

All movements of the rifle should be carried out smartly ; the correct position of the slope is as follows :—

The butt held firmly in the left hand.
The rifle flat on the left shoulder.
Magazine outwards from the body.
The upper part of left arm close to the side.
The lower part horizontal.
The heel of the butt in line with centre of left thigh.

For changing arms the following is the correct method :—

Change Arms. — Pass the left hand up quickly and seize the rifle at the small, fingers and thumb round the stock ; at the same time grasp the butt with the right hand, the first two joints of the fingers grasping the outside of the butt, thumb round the heel.

Two.	Raise the rifle to a perpendicular position and carry it across the body.
Three.	Place it on the right shoulder, guard to the left, thumb round the heel.
Four.	Drop the left hand smartly to the side.
Change Arms.	Pass the right hand up quickly and seize the rifle at the small, fingers and thumb round the stock, at the same time grasp the butt with the left hand, the first two joints of the fingers grasping the outside of the butt, thumb round the toe.
Two.	Raise the rifle to a perpendicular position and carry it across the body.
Three.	Place it on the left shoulder, guard to the left.
Four.	Drop the right hand smartly to the side.

Saluting:

Sentries will (until further orders) never come to the "Present."

When saluting an officer they will come to the "Slope" and will make the salute by carrying the right hand smartly to the small of the butt, forearm horizontal, back of the hand to the front, fingers extended.

Relieving Sentries:

On the approach of the relief the sentry with rifle at the slope will place himself in front of his post. The new sentry with rifle at the slope will fall in on the left of the old sentry facing in the same direction. The old sentry will then give over his orders; the C.P.O. seeing they are correctly given and understood.

The C.P.O. will give the command "Pass." The old sentry will take two paces to his front and turn to the flank from which the relief approached. The new sentry will close two paces to his right. The C.P.O. will give the command "Relief—Quick-march."

When Posted Indoors:

The sentry will stand correctly at ease at his post.

When saluting an officer he will spring smartly to attention and remain still till the officer has passed.

NOTE 1.—Carry out all movements of the rifle smartly.

NOTE 2.—Move about your post smartly.

NOTE 3.—When standing to attention or saluting always look straight to your front.

NOTE 4.—Sentries must not quit their arms, lounge or converse with anyone on any pretence.

NOTE 5.—Sentries moving on their post will always turn outwards when turning about.

LOCAL ORDERS.

I. By day all persons approaching the sentry's post (*except officers* personally known to him) are to be challenged and ordered to show their passes.

II. The following passes entitle bearers to entry provided they explain satisfactorily their business on the station:—

(*a*) Anti-aircraft passes.
(*b*) Office of Works passes signed by Messrs. Frank and Hubert Baines.
(*c*) Post Office telephone passes.

III. In case of doubt or where bearer is not provided with a proper pass the Officer or C.P.O. is to be summoned, and will decide what steps to take. Workmen, &c. carrying out orders should not be turned away simply because they have no pass. The Officer or C.P.O. must use his own initiative as regards this and wherever possible should allow the necessary access, provide a suitable guard, and report the matter to Central.

IV. "Challenges" will be made as follows:—

By Day.—"Halt"!—"State your business"—"Advance and produce your Pass."

By Night.—"Halt! who goes there?"—"State your business"—"Advance and produce your pass."

Sentries should never give the order to "advance" unless satisfied as to the bona fides of the person challenged. If the answer to the challenge is unsatisfactory, the sentry should at once bring his rifle to the position of "on guard," and summon assistance.

II.—DISCIPLINE AND DRILL.

Remember that no body of men can be of any military value without discipline.

Discipline must become an instinct, a second nature to the sailor.

Discipline is produced and maintained by—

(*a*) Constant attention to the smallest details.
(*b*) Never allowing a fault or slackness of any kind to pass unchecked.
(*c*) Drill.

Smartness at drill means good discipline.

Slovenly and indistinct words of command result in slackness and hesitation on the part of the men.

Men should be perfected in one movement before going on to another.

Do not expect your men to drill like guardsmen until they have become efficient in squad and company drill. All movements of the rifle should be carried out with the utmost smartness, never allow a fault to pass uncorrected.

When men in uniform are not on duty they must always carry themselves in a smart manner and be properly dressed.

They must salute all officers.

If smoking when approaching an officer, they must remove their smokes until they have passed.

All officers should make themselves thoroughly acquainted with the names of the different parts of the rifle (*see* Plate I., Rifle and Field Exercises).

They should also know the "General Definitions" on pages 1 and 2, Rifle and Field Exercises.

III.—HINTS ON RIFLE SHOOTING.

1. You cannot shoot well unless in a comfortable position.

2. Be sure your sights are properly adjusted.

3. The correct lying position is as follows:—

   (*a*) Body oblique to line of fire.
   (*b*) Legs well separated.
   (*c*) Heels on ground.
   (*d*) Good bed for the butt.
   (*e*) Firm grip with both hands.

(*f*) Eye well back from the cocking piece.
(*g*) Sights perfectly upright.
(*h*) Elbows closed slightly forwards.

4. Do not pull the trigger, but release it with a squeezing motion of the forefinger and thumb of the right hand.

5. When about to fire, restrain your breathing.

6. The correct aim is as shown :–

IV.—MINIATURE RANGE.

Practices on the Admiralty miniature range take place daily except Saturday and Sunday between the hours of 2.30 p.m. and 4.30 p.m.

Thirty-two men practise a day under their own officers, only eight men being allowed on the range at one time.

A C.P.O. Naval Rating is always present to give instruction.

A register is kept with scores made.

Ten rounds per man are fired.

Those scoring under 70 out of a possible 100 will be required to go through further practice at a later date.

CHAPTER VI.

CONTROL TELEPHONE SYSTEM.

I.—EXPLANATION OF DIAGRAM OF TELEPHONE SYSTEM.

I. The Central Control Exchange Switchboard at Admiralty Arch is in telephone connection with eleven Sub-Control Stations:—

1. St. James' - - -	On the "Loop."
2. Crown Agents - -	
3. Nine Elms - -	
4. Waterloo - - -	
5. Tower - - -	
6. St. Helens - - -	
7. Gresham - - -	

No. 1. Outer Sub-Control.
No. 2. " "
No. 3. " "

II. These Sub-Control Stations are sub-exchanges and are in connection with the various gun and light positions of their Sub-Control.

III. Thus, by means of the switchboard at Sub-Control Stations Central can be placed in direct communication with any gun or light position in any Sub-Control.

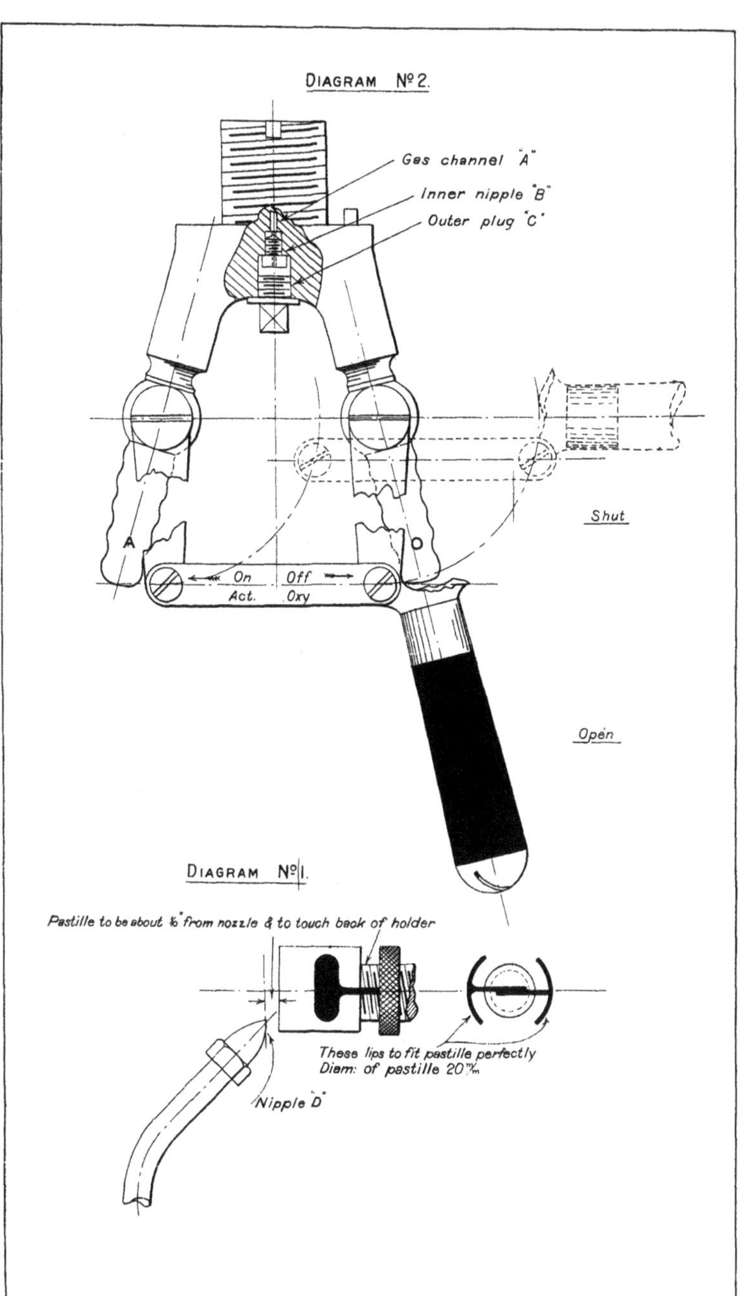

3539-39858-P34. 100. 1.15.
Malby & Sons. Lith.

IV. If, however, the direct line to any Sub-Control (except Outer Sub-Control) is broken down, Central can communicate with that Sub-Control Station (and consequently with any gun or light position in that Sub-Control) by calling up any other Sub-Control Station and being switched through on the Loop Line. Similarly, Sub-Controls can communicate with each other along the Loop Line without calling up Central.

V. The switchboard at all Sub-Controls is uniform, and is very simple to work. It is not, however, adapted to rough usage, and, in a large number of cases, breakdowns which occur are caused by misuse on the part of operators.

VI. Procedure to call up a Station is as follows:—

(A.) Press down the key of that Station for a few seconds, to ring; then lift up the key to the speaking position and carry on your conversation at the No. 1 Instrument.

(B.) If the No. 1 Instrument is in use, press down, as before, the key of the Station you want; then plug the "jack" of the No. 2 instrument into the hole beneath the key, and place the key in the ordinary horizontal position. You can then carry on your conversation at No. 2 Instrument.

VII. To place any two Stations in communication it is only necessary to place the keys of those Stations in the speaking position. The method by which calls of this description are to be made is as follows:—

Example:—Central Control wishes to speak to Great Western through Gresham:—

(A.) Central rings Gresham and asks for Great Western.

(B.) Gresham rings St. James', and asks for Great Western; then places keys to Admiralty and St. James' in speaking position.

(C.) St. James' rings Crown Agents, and asks for Great Western; then places keys to Gresham and Crown Agents in speaking position.

(D.) Crown Agents rings Nine Elms, and asks for Great Western; then places keys to St. James' and Nine Elms in speaking position.

(E.) Nine Elms rings Great Western, assures himself that telephone is being answered; then places Crown Agents and Great Western keys in speaking position.

NOTE.—The whole operation sketched out above should not take more than 30 seconds.

VIII. The following notes should be carefully studied by all officers and operators:—

(*a*) The rapidity with which messages can be passed through the system depends upon the efficiency of the operators.

(*b*) The instruments are as good as they well can be. Alleged "breakdowns" are in almost every case caused by the inefficiency of the operators.

(*c*) Messages given over the telephone should always be passed on absolutely word for word. Mistakes will always creep in unless this is done.

(*d*) Telephone operators should always be restrained from commenting aloud on messages received. Other operators may be on the line at the same time, and ejaculations expressing surprise, disgust, or incomprehension merely serve to muddle other people.

(*e*) Whenever possible any message received should be written down at the same time. This prevents mistakes and is an aid to memory.

II.—EXTRACT FROM ORDERS FOR SUB-CONTROL TELEPHONE OPERATORS.

I. The telephone operator should never take over the watch unless he is sure he understands all about the switchboard and what to do in all emergencies.

II. He should always commence his watch by testing his telephone connections to the stations in his Sub-Control, and to the Sub-Controls to which he is connected by the Loop Line. (His line to Central Control will be tested by the Central Operator.)

III. He should know by heart the names of all stations in the London Defence, and should be able at once to make any connection by the shortest route along the Loop Line.

IV. He should never touch his alarm bell push to the other stations in his Sub-Control unless the Central bell rings, or unless directly ordered to do so by the Sub-Control Officer, in which case he will act *at once and will not wait to ask questions.*

V. When the main alarm bell sounds he will proceed as follows, not forgetting that *every second is of importance* :—

(*a*) Plug in his second telephone instrument to Central Control, place it to his ear and *never* let go of it till "Secure" is ordered. (The switch remains *horizontal* for this instrument.)

(*b*) Ring alarm bell to all stations on his Sub-Control and to officers' and men's rooms.

(*c*) Place the telephone instrument in the Sub-Control Officers' position in connection with the stations of his Sub-Control (switches up).

(He will not touch the "Loop Line" switches unless his line to Central is broken down, in which case he will receive instructions from Central *viâ* the next Sub-Control on the Loop Line.)

(*d*) Stand by to pass verbally (by voice pipe or otherwise) all information and orders received from Central to his Sub-Control Officer.

VI. When called he will always answer with the name of his Sub-Control only. He should never use the expressions "Hallo," or "Are you there?" They waste time.

VII. He will *always repeat all orders received.* If he does this, he saves a lot of talking, and the Central operator knows that he has got his orders correctly.

If he is standing near the voice pipe or within speaking distance of his officer, his repetition of the order will inform both the officer and Central at the same time.

VIII. He must *never forget* that a mistake due to his ignorance or carelessness (an un-made switch or a wrong connection, &c.) may, in case of an attack, have the most serious consequence by causing confusion and perhaps failure in his portion of the London Defence.

IX. In case of doubt he should *always* call his Sub-Control Officer. Definite signalling lights, reports of aircraft in the vicinity, &c., should always be reported to the Sub-Control Officer immediately, so that he may decide upon what steps to take.

In case of emergency, the operator must not wait till the officer comes up, but inform Central *at once*, and if he thinks necessary, ring the alarm bell.

Telephone Operators at Guns and Light Positions.

The above orders apply generally to all telephone operators. Operators at stations will answer with the name of their stations. On the alarm bell being sounded, they will sound their local alarms, and remain at their telephone instruments until the "Secure" is ordered.

III.—TELEPHONE QUARTERS.

An exercise known as "Telephone Quarters" will take place twice daily, once between the hours of 8—12 a.m. and once between 8 p.m. and midnight. This exercise is for the purpose of familiarising the operators at Sub-Control Stations and gun and light positions with their instruments, and insuring correct and immediate passing of all orders.

The exercises will be carried out as follows:—

(1) All Sub-Controls will be warned by telephone "Prepare for Telephone Quarters."

(2) On receiving this order the Duty Sub-Control Officer or the Chief P.O. in charge of the station (or for the purpose of exercise any member of the crew who may be ordered to do so) will take the Sub-Control Officer's position. The telephone operator at Sub-Controls will plug in his instrument to the Admiralty and provide himself with pencil and signal pad. The stations on the Sub-Control will be warned by the Duty Sub-Control Officer (or his substitute) to "prepare for Telephone Quarters." The telephone operators of the gun and light positions will then keep their ear and provide themselves with paper and pencil.

(3) As soon as this warning has been received by all stations and they are ready for the exercises, each station will report individually to its Sub-Control "ready for exercise," and as soon as all stations of each Sub-Control have reported, the Sub-Control Officer (or his substitute) will order the telephone operator at his Sub-Control station to ring up and inform Admiralty.

(4) The exercise will commence as soon as all Sub-Controls report "Ready," the first order being "Telephone Quarters."

(5) A set series of orders will then be passed from Central Control, Admiralty, and all operators will write these down as they are passed. The Sub-Control Officers (or their substitutes), for the purpose of these exercises, acting purely as repeating Centres and passing on the message, word for word.

(6) No order will ever be repeated. No station will be addressed by name except under exceptional circumstances.

(7) On the completion of the exercises (on the order "Exercise finished") the copies of the orders received at the Sub-Control Stations and at the gun and light positions, as written down by the operators, are to be collected as early as convenient by the respective Sub-Control Officers, who will forward all exercises received to the Duty Telephone Officer, Anti-Aircraft Central Exchange.

(8) Percentage marks will be given for these exercises as for signalling exercises in ships, and these

marks will be posted up weekly by the Sub-Control Officers for the information of all concerned.

(9) The name and rating of operators is to be clearly written on all exercises when sent in.

(10) This exercise will frequently be varied by a partial breakdown of communication (for exercise), and the consequent passing of orders by Loop Line.

NOTE.—Forenoon exercises will affect gun stations only. "8 p.m.-midnight" all stations.

---

u 26597

CHAPTER VII.

SIGNALLING INSTRUCTION.

SIGNALLING.

It being impracticable to pass the whole Corps through signalling classes at Headquarters, signalling instruction will be carried on independently at stations. It is hoped that among the crews of each station there are some members who already possess sufficient knowledge of signalling, and who will be willing to instruct the crews up to the point, after which practice is all that is necessary to attain a useful working speed. Such volunteer instructors as are not yet expert enough will attend classes at Headquarters until they are sufficiently so. Stations will be inspected and their progress noted.

With a view to simplicity, the Morse system has been adopted for day and night use, and the signals are reproduced below, together with the semaphore alphabet, for the convenience of those who may desire to learn it on their own account.

Morse Alphabet.

A	· —	N	— ·
B	— · · ·	O	— — —
C	— · — ·	P	· — — ·
D	— · ·	Q	— — · —
E	·	R	· — ·
F	· · — ·	S	· · ·
G	— — ·	T	—
H	· · · ·	U	· · —
I	· ·	V	· · · —
J	· — — —	W	· — —
K	— · —	X	— · · —
L	· — · ·	Y	— · — —
M	— —	Z	— — · ·

Numerals.

The following are the Morse Symbols for Figures, which, if used, should be proceded by the Numeral Sign (· · — · · ·).

1. · — — — —
2. · · — — —
3. · · · — —
4. · · · · —
5. · · · · ·
6. — · · · ·
7. — — · · ·
8. — — — · ·
9. — — — — ·
0. — — — — —

The procedure to be followed in sending messages will be as follows :—

The sending station will call up the receiving station by sending the latter's name in the following abbreviated form until answered :—

Central	C	Green Park	GP
Charing Cross	CX	Foreign Office	FO
Crown Agents	CA	Waterloo	WT
Lambeth	LB	Newington	NT
Hyde Park	HP	Temple	TL
Gresham	GR	Wakefield	WK
Salisbury	SY	Imrie	IR
Tower	TW	Wapping	WP
Nine Elms	NE	Great Western	GW
St. Helens	ST	Cannon Street	CS
St. James	LL		

The receiving station will then reply by repeating its code letters as above, and if ready to receive will give the letter G, on receipt of which the sending station will proceed with the message separating the address from the body by a full stop. Each word will be acknowledged by sending letter T. If no acknowledgment is received, the sending station will repeat the last word and proceed. If repetition of any particular word or words is required, receiving station will give the repeat signal I.M.I., and then W.A. (word after) or A.A. (all after) the appropriate preceding word. When the message is finished, sending station will give the general stop signal, and the receiving station will give "understand."

The following points should be attended to:—

(A) Do not send too slowly at early stages, give as much interval as is desired between letters, but too slow sending leads to letters being identified by the number of dots and dashes they contain, and not by the general effect of the letters as a whole.

(B) In flag waving form each letter by a continuous wave of the flag, and do not cut it up into lengths.

(C) In lamp signalling send the dots firmly to allow of the lamp lighting up properly if electric light is used, but keep the dots as short as possible subject to this.

(D) Pay particular attention to keeping the flag clear.

(E) Do not attempt to learn the Morse alphabet by the aid of rhymes or opposite letters or any other method than that of working steadily through it.

(F) The lamp employed must be shielded by a tube or similar device so that the light is only visible to the station for which it is intended.

(G) All officers are expected to make themselves expert in signalling, so that they may be able to instruct their men and read messages without having to rely on other people.

CHAPTER VIII.

INSTRUCTIONS FOR THE USE OF THE DIRECTION CORRECTOR FITTED AT ALL GUN, LIGHT AND LOOK-OUT STATIONS IN LONDON.

I. As the instrument is very susceptible to wet, it should be kept under cover except when in use, and should always be wiped over after being used at night.

II. Great care should be taken not to break the glass or damage the instrument in any way, as no replacements can be made.

III. The instrument is intended to act as the "Standard Compass" of the station, and allows an immediate rough correction for simultaneously concentrating the attention of all stations to a given point.

IV. The instrument is the same at all stations, with the exception that the sighting bar pivot is placed above the spot on the chart representing the position of the station.

V. The accuracy of the instrument absolutely depends on its being placed accurately North and South on its support. and it is worse than useless unless it fits correctly in its sockets.

VI. On seeing suspicious lights, aircraft, &c. aim the sighting bar at the object and get it as correctly as possible over the front and back sight. Report to Central (Admiralty) the point at which the direction rod cuts the edge of the chart and the side which it is on, thus "South. 27" or "West 14," &c., also the angle of elevation or depression (from scale on side of sighting tube). (It is obvious that great inaccuracy may be caused by the object being *within* the area shown on the chart (the range of visibility will probably prevent anything outside this area being seen, and in that case the angular error between various stations will be fairly small). If, however, two stations see the same thing, the "Key Chart" at the Admiralty will allow an immediate and accurate bearing to be passed to each individual station.)

VII. On receiving orders from the Admiralty or from your Sub-Control to concentrate gun or light at a given point—(*a*) At gun stations the officer or operator turns the direction rod to the numbered square indicated and then reads off the *compass* bearing of that square. This compass bearing he passes on to the gun and the gun is immediately laid upon that bearing by means of the compass point painted on the handrails or shutters. (*b*) At light stations the operator carries out the same routine. If an angle of elevation for the light be given, he places his sight tube at that elevation and his direction rod on the square, watching carefully through the tube and directing the light until the point of the beam of the light appears through the tube when the light should be as nearly as possible on the spot desired. (The distance between gun and instrument is so small as to be negligible.)

VIII. The following rather obvious points are worth noting :—

The direction corrector supplies—

(*a*) A chart of London which will permit the operator to judge the probable cause of "Searchlights,"

&c., if over electric railways, trams, or from the direction of other stations.

(*b*) The exact direction and distance from the operator of all other gun and light positions in London. It has been impossible to put in the names of these, but operators can readily learn which is which—

Guns are shown thus— ▣
Lights are shown thus— ⊙

(*c*) A correct compass which allows the operator to direct his gun or light to any point observed by himself with the direction corrector—

(N.B.—Always pass the *Direction Corrector bearing* (*i.e.*, East 34. North 22) to *Central*, the *compass bearing* to the gun or light.)

(*d*) A means of spotting the bearing and elevation of suspicious lights, &c., by night, jotting them down and definitely settling their exact position by day.

(*e*) A method of focussing a light exactly on a given point.

IX. It is suggested that officers should provide themselves with pocket flash-lamps to facilitate the reading of the instrument at night, as the hurricane lamps (being supplied) are rather clumsy.

FUZE SCALE FOR 6-PR. Q.F. HOTCHKISS AND NORDENFELDT GUNS.

Based on Practice of 18.12.14.

Projectile :—Common Shell.
Fuze :—T. and P. No. 56.
Charge :—8 ozs. 11¼ drs., Cordite M.D. size 4½.

Range.	Time of Flight.	Fuze Set.	Range.	Time of Flight.	Fuze Set.
Yards.	Seconds.		Yards.	Seconds.	
100	0·18	—	2,600	6·50	8
200	0·36	—	2,700	6·83	8½
300	0·55	—	2,800	7·16	9
400	0·75	—	2,900	7·50	9½
500	0·96	—	3,000	7·84	10
600	1·18	—	3,100	8·18	10½
700	1·40	¼	3,200	8·53	10¾
800	1·62	½	3,300	8·88	11¼
900	1·84	1	3,400	9·24	11¾
1,000	2·07	1½	3,500	9·60	12¼
1,100	2·30	1¾	3,600	9·97	12¾
1,200	2·54	2	3,700	10·34	13¼
1,300	2·78	2½	3,800	10·70	13¾
1,400	3·03	2¾	3,900	11·07	14¼
1,500	3·28	3¼	4,000	11·44	14½
1,600	3·53	3½	4,100	11·82	15
1,700	3·79	4	4,200	12·20	15½
1,800	4·06	4½	4,300	12·58	16
1,900	4·35	4¾	4,400	12·96	16½
2,000	4·64	5¼	4,500	13·34	17
2,100	4·93	5¾	4,600	13·73	17½
2,200	5·23	6	4,700	14·13	18
2,300	5·54	6½			
2,400	5·85	7			
2,500	6·18	7½			

FUZE SCALE FOR 3-IN. Q.F. H.A. GUN.

Based on Practice of 14.3.13.

Fuze :—T. and P. No. 81 or No. 84.
Charge :—2 lbs. 10 ozs., Cordite M.D. size 11.

Range.	Time of Flight.	Fuze Set.	Range.	Time of Flight.	Fuze Set.	Range.	Time of Flight.	Fuze Set.
Yards.	Seconds.		Yards.	Seconds.		Yards.	Seconds.	
100	0·12	0·8	3,100	5·88	5·5	6,100	16·32	13·5
200	0·24	0·9	3,200	6·17	5·8	6,200	16·74	13·8
300	0·36	1·0	3,300	6·46	6·0	6,300	17·17	14·1
400	0·49	1·1	3,400	6·76	6·3	6,400	17·60	14·4
500	0·62	1·2	3,500	7·06	6·5	6,500	18·04	14·7
600	0·75	1·3	3,600	7·37	6·7	6,600	18·48	15·0
700	0·89	1·5	3,700	7·68	7·0	6,700	18·93	15·3
800	1·03	1·6	3,800	7·99	7·2	6,800	19·39	15·7
900	1·17	1·7	3,900	8·30	7·5	6,900	19·85	16·0
1,000	1·32	1·8	4,000	8·61	7·7	7,000	20·32	16·4
1,100	1·48	2·0	4,100	8·93	8·0	7,100	20·80	16·7
1,200	1·64	2·1	4,200	9·26	8·2	7,200	21·29	17·1
1,300	1·81	2·2	4,300	9·59	8·5	7,300	21·79	17·5
1,400	1·98	2·4	4,400	9·93	8·7	7,400	22·30	17·8
1,500	2·16	2·5	4,500	10·27	9·0	7,500	22·82	18·2
1,600	2·34	2·7	4,600	10·62	9·2	7,600	23·35	18·5
1,700	2·53	2·8	4,700	10·97	9·5	7,700	23·88	18·9
1,800	2·73	3·0	4,800	11·33	9·8	7,800	24·42	19·3
1,900	2·93	3·1	4,900	11·69	10·0	7,900	24·96	19·7
2,000	3·14	3·3	5,000	12·05	10·3	8,000	25·50	20·1
2,100	3·36	3·5	5,100	12·42	10·6	8,100	26·05	20·5
2,200	3·59	3·7	5,200	12·79	10·9	8,200	26·61	20·9
2,300	3·82	3·9	5,300	13·16	11·1	8,300	27·18	21·3
2,400	4·06	4·0	5,400	13·54	11·4	8,400	27·77	21·7
2,500	4·30	4·2	5,500	13·93	11·7			
2,600	4·55	4·4	5,600	14·32	12·0			
2,700	4·81	4·6	5,700	14·71	12·3			
2,800	5·07	4·8	5,800	15·11	12·6			
2,900	5·33	5·1	5,900	15·51	12·9			
3,000	5·60	5·3	6,000	15·91	13·2			

ADDENDA TO NOTES ON ATTACK.

At the same time, if the guns require more light, he should use his own discretion as to the employment of those lights at his disposal most likely to help him.

VII. During an attack the Sub-Control Officer should never lose sight of the fact that where there is one airship there will probably be others approaching, and that immediately he has brought the airship he is attacking to earth or she gets beyond range, he should switch off his lights and prepare for further action.

VIII. Where a Sub-Control Officer is controlling guns other than that at his own station, he must keep a sharp eye on their shooting, and if he considers the fire of any particular gun is wild, he should never hesitate to order that gun to cease firing.

IX. In case of attack by aeroplane the guns are not to be used *unless supplied with incendiary ammunition or shrapnel.* Sub-Control Officers whose guns are without this ammunition will, therefore, rely entirely upon rifle fire from their gun and light positions. The 45 Martini rifles, as well as the Lee-Metfords, may be used for this purpose.

X. Duty Sub-Control Officers having located an airship at night, but being unable to see it, may switch on a single light for as short a time as possible, for verification purposes before telephoning to Central, but they should use this power with considerable discretion.

XI. Officers of gun positions receiving the order to "Commence," and being unable to see the target, should hold their fire and inform their Sub-Control Officer.

XII. Officers should never wait for the order to "Cease fire" if they consider the target out of range. They should act on their own responsibility and inform their Sub-Control Officer.

XIII. As regards rifle fire, officers should continually practise their crews in concerted fire with a view of gaining the maximum effect.

Lightning Source UK Ltd.
Milton Keynes UK
UKHW03f1812030418
320464UK00001B/7/P

9 781847 348258